This Book Belongs To:

_____

Dedicated to Mishay, Aarya, Rishi and Ravi:
Let your curiosity take you to all the places we've only dreamed.

ISBN Hardcover 978-1-7334752-2-8
ISBN Paperback 978-1-7334752-3-5

Published in the United States by Imaginarium Press, LLC.
Annabelle & Aiden is a trademark of Joseph Becker.

Annabelle & Aiden

OH MY GODS!

A HISTORY OF BELIEF

Written by J.R. Becker

Illustrated by Marissa Napolitano

"I would suggest that there is no such thing as a new religion. Religions are like ice cores. In each, one can find layer upon layer of past belief." - Matthew Kneale

"Whether you believe in one God or many gods or no god, it is we who have fashioned God in our image, not the other way around...so everything good or bad about our religions is merely a reflection of everything that is good or bad about us. Our desires become god's desires. Our actions become god's actions. We fashion our religions and cultures according to our own human urges, all the while convincing ourselves that those urges are god's. That explains why...religion has been a force both for boundless good and for unspeakable evil; why two people can approach the same scripture at the same time and come away with two radically opposing interpretations of it. Indeed, most of the religious conflicts that continue to roil our world arise from our innate, unconscious desire to make ourselves the apotheosis of what God is and what God wants, whom God loves and whom God hates." - Reza Aslan, *God: A Human History*

Annabelle & Aiden played,
on the grass one cloudy day.
Aiden held a plastic toy,
and he made the small tree say,

"I'm a happy, tall old tree.
I'm at peace, and I'm so wise.
I've got branches for my arms,
and small tree knots for my eyes."

2

Annabelle then paused and asked,
"If these play toys are not real,
why does everyone pretend
they can think and talk and feel?"

"Oh, like how this car is sad?
I'm not sure. That's how we play."

But then Tardigrade Tom said,
"Humans grew to think this way...

As we first formed long ago,
and our brains all slowly grew,
soon we grasped that others had
thoughts and feelings like we do.

To conceive how others felt!
This was something very new.
But we took this way too far,
thinking **things** had feelings too.

Religions' origins? Explanations abound.
Theory of mind: we evolved to view others
the way we view ourselves, but a side effect
of this is the compulsion to view nonhumans
in this fashion as well, such as animals and objects.

2) HADD (hypersensitive agency detection
device): we evolved to detect (human-like)
agency behind any unexplained event,
such as a predator behind a rustling bush.

3) Dreams: ancient man dreamt, sometimes of
dead relatives, causing them to conclude souls
still live, apart from bodies.
Thus, a spiritual realm.

We thought *everything* could feel.
Rocks and clouds and ants and trees.
We thought mountains all had souls,
as did rivers, sun, and seas.

ANIMISM

As we fretted over food,
hunting animals as prey,
we asked creatures for their help
through their spirits, in this way:

We climbed deep inside dark caves,
drew their spirits on the stone,
breathed the smoke in from their fires,
played on flutes made from their bone.

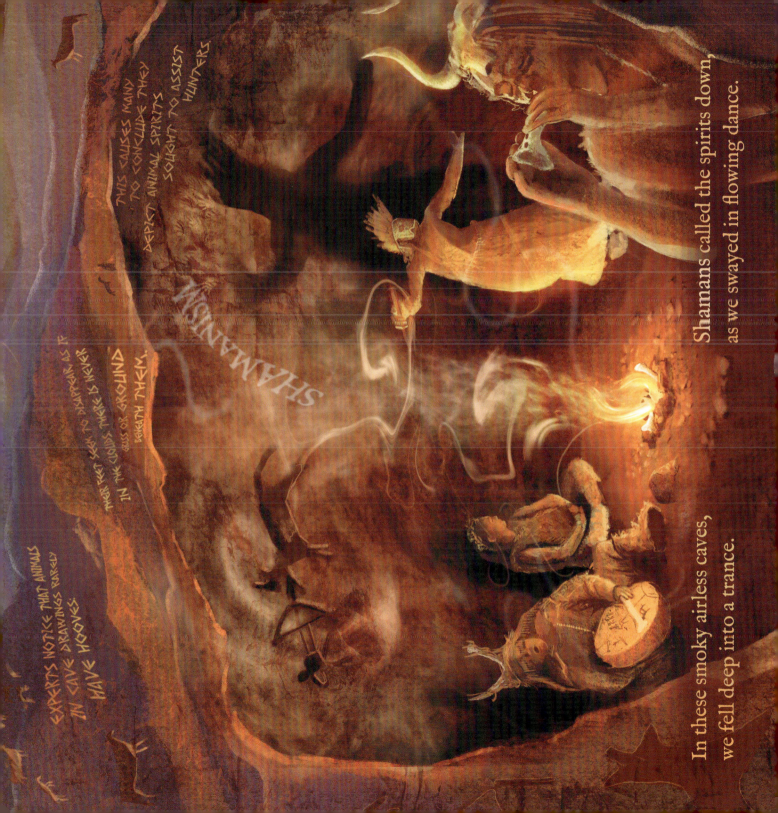

SHAMANISM

THIS CAUSES MANY TO CONCLUDE THEY DEPICT ANIMAL SPIRITS SOUGHT TO ASSIST HUNTERS.

EXPERTS NOTICE THAT ANIMALS IN CAVE DRAWINGS RARELY HAVE HOOVES; THEIR FEET SEEM TO DISAPPEAR, AS IF IN THE CLOUDS. THERE IS NEVER GRASS OR GROUND BENEATH THEM.

Shamans called the spirits down, as we swayed in flowing dance.

In these smoky airless caves, we fell deep into a trance.

We changed spirits into gods,
who we thought controlled our fates.
Making them relatable,
we assigned them human traits:

ANU

MESOPOTAMIA

gave them offerings for food,
and assigned them families,
gave them temples as a home,
names and personalities.

The earliest flood stories are written,
such as the Sumerian Epic of Atrahasis,
which will be retold and modified
many times by future religions
claiming it as their own.

ENLIL

8

Like Enlil, the god of storms.
Or his dad, sky god Anu.
Aya's spouse, sun god Shamash,
who was later called Utu.

We made thousands of these gods,
each with temples filled with food.
So we learned to farm and write,
to keep track of all accrued.

From Hunting to Farming
Planning & construction
of huge temples (like
Göbekli Tepe) takes years
and huge workforces,

requiring a steady food
supply in the same place.

Many think this is what
drove us to settle, and
transform from hunter-
gatherers to farmers.

MANY THINK THE INVENTION OF WRITING TOOK OFF
TO RECORD TEMPLE TRANSACTIONS, WHICH ALSO
SPROUTED BUSINESS AND THE CONCEPT OF
ACCOUNTANCY, WHICH IN TURN SPAWNED THE IDEA
OF SACRIFICE AS A TRANSACTION WITH THE GODS.

9

But as life got easier,
and we learned how to get by,
our fears changed from **present threats**,
to what happens **when we die.**

So to keep their bodies clean,
we all mummified our kings.
Then we placed them in huge tombs
buried with their favorite things,

EGYPT

underworld

The first monotheist on record, the Egyptian king Akhenaten led a harsh campaign for Egyptians to discard their many gods and worship Aten only. It didn't last; when he died, the Egyptians made sure his ideas died with him.

AKHENATEN

for the afterlife we dreamed,
where we fly across the sky,
side by side with gods like Ra,
Isis, Shu, or Khen-tekh-tai.

GREECE

HERMES

ATLAS

HADES

POSEIDON

METIS

ZEUS

It was prophesied that Metis would bear powerful children who would eventually overthrow Zeus. To avoid this, Zeus tricked her into turning herself into a fly. Then he swallowed her.

And in Greece, we traded tales of the gods that were quite wild. Like when Zeus swallowed his wife so she wouldn't have a child.

But he got a headache, and
birthed Athena from his head.
If you thought that **yours** were weird,
try these families instead!

13

ZOROASTRIANISM

HVAR KSATA

ATAR

In Iran, we worshipped gods
like Hvar Ksata and Atar.
But one man there disagreed,
so he left and wandered far.

'Till a river blocked his path.
Here, he claimed something quite odd:
through a light, a vision came,
telling him there's just <u>one</u> god.

The first prophet of our time.
Zoroaster was his name.
He spoke of a golden age,
but these teachings gave him fame:

AHURA MAZDA

ZOROASTER

Monotheism is born! But it won't last.
Zoroastrianism will later change into a dualist religion.
Today, it is one of the oldest surviving religions,
with about 200,000 members, mostly in Iran and India.

that "Ahura Mazda" is
the sole god anyone needs.
And he taught to fight evil
with good words,
    good thoughts,
        good deeds.

15

These ideas reached India,
and the afterlife changed to
being reborn after death,
every time as someone new.

HINDUISM

But this changed to benefit
just the rich folks at the top.
Like Siddhartha, a young prince,
who said, **"This has got to stop!"**

He left home alone one night,
left his newborn son and wife.
He saw sickness and old age
for the first time in his life.

Siddharta didn't like how reincarnation upholds India's
caste system, as people in lower castes were seen as
sinners, and lived only to be reincarnated into a
higher caste. He rejected this exclusivity of heaven.

bodhi tree

Sitting underneath a tree,
he began to meditate,
until answers came to him.
It took **49 days straight!**

He taught, "Heaven is a state
anybody could achieve,
when we do not focus on
things we haven't yet received."

BUDDHISM

He died around the age of 80,
his last words were
"Believe not because an old book
is produced as an authority,"

nor because your father,
or everyone around you, believes it.

Rather
"test everything,
try everything,
and **then** believe it."

JUDAISM

ASSYRIA

PERSIAN GULF

"Jews were committed polytheists; it was only after various assaults by Babylonian and Assyrian armies..."

Also, Middle Eastern tribes worshipped many gods as well: Baal, Ashera, Yahweh, Yam, Moloch, Inara, and El.

BABYLONIA

ISRAEL

DEAD SEA

JERUSALEM

JUDAH

...and their temple's destruction, which they considered to be by the god Marduk, that they decided to repent and say the prophets urging them to chose Yahweh as their only god, over the others, such as El or Elohim (which actually translates into 'God.') Still, the change was gradual, as the gods slowly merged together, their names, such as Yahweh-Elohim.

MEDITERRANEAN SEA

Israelites praised those gods too, all while split in two nations, both of which suffered attacks from nearby populations.

When their temple got destroyed, to survive, there was one way: they united into one, choosing one god, named Yahweh.

RED SEA

Zoroastrianism, and flood stories from

Jews also merged their texts, borrowing ideas such as messiah from

Gilgamesh and other sources.

ARABIA

And they merged their texts as well,
adding stories from the past.
For the first time, the idea
of a single god would last.

Monotheism was not new: both Zoroaster and Egyptian pharaoh
Akhenaten were strict monotheists. However, their monotheism
died with them. This time, it would last.

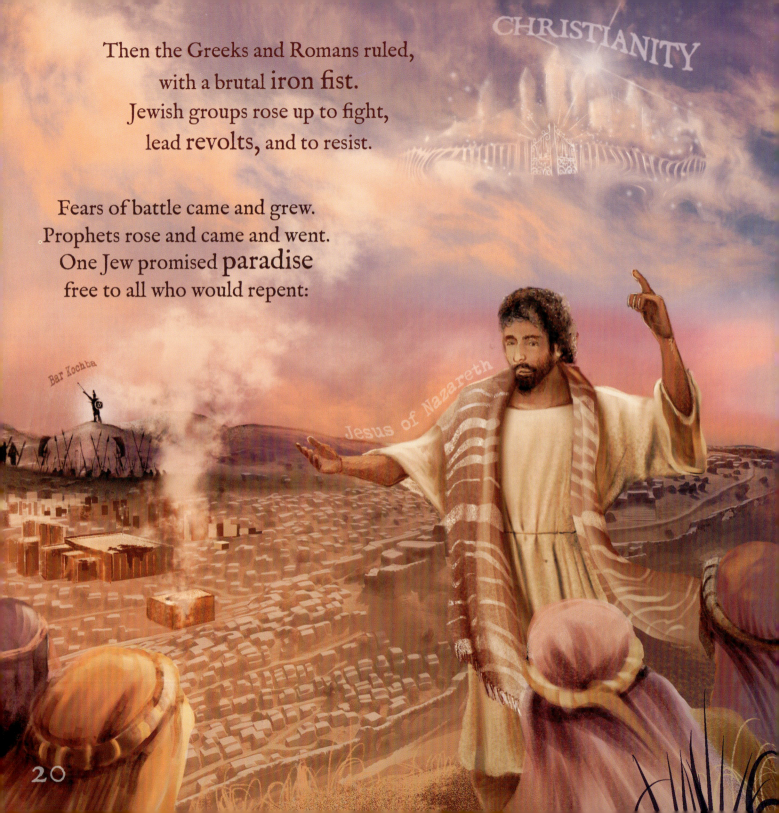

Then the Greeks and Romans ruled,
with a brutal **iron fist**.
Jewish groups rose up to fight,
lead **revolts**, and to resist.

Fears of battle came and grew.
Prophets rose and came and went.
One Jew promised **paradise**
free to all who would repent:

CHRISTIANITY

Bar Kochba

Jesus of Nazareth

20

"A pure Kingdom of Heaven!
After war will <u>end</u> <u>these</u> <u>times</u>."
Rome did not like this at all:
so they tried him for his crimes.

Then he died, but days later,
some claim something very odd.
They said he came back to life,
since he was the son of god.

21

Prophets said all different things.
People argued, even warred,
over whether gods exist:
whether two or three or more.

Like in Mecca. In this town,
hundreds of stone idols stood.
But one man would not bow down
even though folks said he should.

Ancient Mecca held the Kaaba, a sanctuary where 360 idols stood.

Kaaba

ISLAM

So he left to meditate,
in a cave not far away.
Then he claimed an angel came,
and that he had heard it say,

Gabriel

"God is one, as others taught.
All will end, as Jesus said.
He'll return, when trumpets play.
That's when God will **raise the dead.**"

Muhammad

In Islamic eschatology, Jesus will return to fight Gog and Magog and establish peace and justice on earth.

23

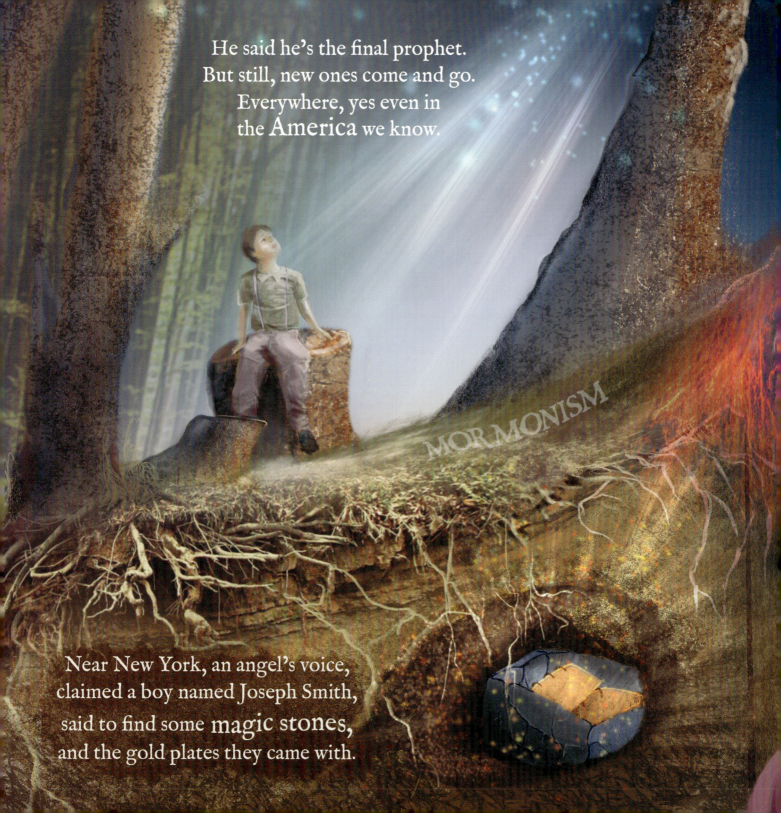

He said he's the final prophet.
But still, new ones come and go.
Everywhere, yes even in
the America we know.

MORMONISM

Near New York, an angel's voice,
claimed a boy named Joseph Smith,
said to find some magic stones,
and the gold plates they came with.

A Montana writer claimed
that some aliens were dropped
in volcanoes, and their souls
have escaped and must be stopped.

25

Annabelle & Aiden thought,
gazing in a nearby pond.
Their reflections all looked back,
causing Aiden to respond,

"All the gods we ever praised,
all the heavens, and the hells,
promises of afterlives,
are just stories of **ourselves**:

from our earliest concerns,
needing rain and food and crops,
to our questions, why we're here,
where we go after it stops.

Gods reflect our governments,
and our kings and families,
our ideas of right and wrong,
and our quirks and jealousies.

Now some folks believe in god.
Others say there's two or more.
Some don't think there's any, but
here's one thing we know **for sure...**

They're a part of our shared past.
They bring out our best and worst.
So, to learn about ourselves,
we could study our gods first.

29

SPECIAL THANKS TO Katie Weaver, Eleanor Ainsley Chatfield, Kodi, Charlotte, and Adeline, Sylus Schmidt, Spencer Schmidt, John Rory Stuart, Andrew, Cameron & Whitney, and Alicia Montgomery, Emma Catherine, Seanna Lyon, Oscar Lyon, Seraphina & Coraline Hoffman, Thomas Krautkramer and Draco Krautkramer, Henry Finn Austin, Phoebe Rose Austin, Oliver Claude Bulleck, Carissa Longo, Charlotte Churchill, Martin Walls, J. David Lowe, Elias Totleben, Julian Totleben, Lila Beren, Pam Solomon and Steve Solomon, Mason Michael Miller, Chandler Aaron Richard Simpson, Wiley Kueper, Halston Kueper, Didi Kueper, Charlie Kueper, Siena & Frankie, James & Tristan, The Crittenden Family, MistressPrime, Gorman-Sortland Family, The Ayres Family, Wesley Carpenter, Declan Carpenter, Anne & Drew Deans, Elliot Abell, Jean Qiu-Wang, Hudson, Channing, Ondine Darcyl, Anais Darcyl Kudler, Donald Kudler, Greyson Lee Wilson, Alayna Leaira Wilson, Jaxon Xavier Spillers, John Kindy, Nevaeh Madison Rose Brace, Georgia Faith Brace, Elia Adraei, Joshua B. Erdin, S. Nigel Rogers, Greg Lynn, Curtis Family, Draughn Family, The Rostler Family, Ken McKnight, Henry, James, and William Kent, E.L.K, Anita Phagan, Eiselt Family, Harper + Micah, Mathilda Rohan, Corey Walther, Persephone Taylor / Osiris Taylor / Nyx Taylor, Carlyle Sherstad Summit Sherstad Ella Anderson, Brandon Rohe, Myra O'Neill-Rohe, Antigone Rohe, Amelia & Ryland Sinden, Oona Mae Baker, Amalia.L. Rego, Ian Hong, Ken Ledbetter, Rick Goheen, Lincoln Simms, Maximus Rolando Ghirarduzzi, Nova Rae Ghirarduzzi, Beau & Hudson Green, Diane Ruth Freeman, Damon Stewart, Jonas Stewart, and Silas Stewart, Steven Hosford, Catherine Durham, Mason Griffee and Jacklynn Griffee, Oliver Belski, Cool Scratch, The Braskat Arellanes Family, Kieran M.Z. Wood, Katia Aryeh, Ian Grey, Alec Kristi, Jean Qiu-Wang, Craig Johnston, Sariah and Sophia Darks, Helena & Desmond Lindsay, Lucia Carolina Zaldivar, Julie Daellenbach, Karen Dhyanchand, Steven Carter, Elizabeth Mayberry, Meaghan & Joe Brassey, Eliana Moreno, Xiara Moreno, Brandon Loncar, Jerry Napolitano, Faeryn Elara Duronslet, The Olivotto Family, Eva & Eddy Allen, Thomas Fyffe, David Lars Chamberlain, Aeden and Sagan Smith, Mr. Jay, Hailey, Emma, Na'amah & Ellah, Cheryl Lynn Ngo, Brandi Reader, Lucia Cobos, Coralea Cobos, William Smith & Family, Stephanie Haines, TeamPayne, Chuck Robinson, Maverick Medina and Felix Medina, and Ben Atlas Wolber

Grab Our Other Titles at *AnnabelleAndAiden.com*

"A beautiful, whimsical, and *deeply important book* for kids of all ages!"
- *Cara Santa Maria,* host of *Talk Nerdy* Podcast, co-author of *The Skeptic's Guide To The Universe*

"A great book. *Very smart. And kind.*"
— *Penn Jillette,* author of *God, No!,* comedian, magician of *Penn & Teller*

"Does an exemplary job of *explaining the origins of life* as we know it *to very young minds.* Heck, it could probably even teach a thing or two to their folks." - *Bill Nye Film*

"What a stunning & *refreshing set of books!* The exact words & tone to reach into a child's heart and brain and bring out such bliss & beauty. A wonderful addition to our family library!"
- *Mayim Bialik,* PhD, actress, author, and neuroscientist.

"*Beautifully illustrated* books for children that opens their minds and hearts to the wonders of science. Any child who reads it will find themselves *mesmerized, enlightened, and smiling.*"
- *Chip Walter,* National Geographic Fellow and author of *Last Ape Standing: The Seven-Million-Year Story of How and Why We Survived*